Discover
the New You

COLOSSIANS

New Community Bible Study Series

Exodus: Journey Toward God
Acts: Build Community
Romans: Find Freedom
Philippians: Run the Race
Colossians: Discover the New You
James: Live Wisely
1 Peter: Stand Strong
1 John: Love Each Other
Parables: Imagine Life God's Way
Sermon on the Mount 1: Connect with God
Sermon on the Mount 2: Connect with Others
Revelation: Experience God's Power

BILL HYBELS

WITH KEVIN & SHERRY HARNEY

New Community
KNOWING. LOVING. SERVING. CELEBRATING.

Discover
the New You

COLOSSIANS

WILLOW
Willow Creek Resources

ZONDERVAN™

GRAND RAPIDS, MICHIGAN 49530 USA

ZONDERVAN™

Colossians: Discover the New You
Copyright © 1999 by the Willow Creek Association

Requests for information should be addressed to:

Zondervan, *Grand Rapids, Michigan 49530*

ISBN: 0-310-22769-0

Interior design by Sherri Hoffman

Printed in the United States of America

06 07 /❖ EP/ 14 13

New Community Bible Study Series   6

Introduction   11

Session 1

A New Look at the Church—Colossians 1:1–14   15

Session 2

A New Look at Jesus—Colossians 1:15–27   24

Session 3

A New Foundation—Colossians 1:28–2:23   33

Session 4

A Whole New You—Colossians 3:1–17   42

Session 5

A New Look at Relationships—
Colossians 3:18–4:1   50

Session 6

A New Voice—Colossians 4:2–18   58

Leader's Notes   67

New Community
BIBLE STUDY SERIES

God has created us for community. This need is built into the very fiber of our being, the DNA of our spirit. As Christians, our deepest desire is to see the truth of God's Word as it influences our relationship with others. We long for a dynamic encounter with God's Word, intimate closeness with His people, and radical transformation of our lives. But how can we accomplish those three difficult tasks?

The New Community Bible Study Series creates a place for all of this to happen. In-depth Bible study, community-building opportunities, and life-changing applications are all built into every session of this small group study series.

How to Build Community

How do we build a strong, healthy Christian community? The whole concept for this study grows out of a fundamental understanding of Christian community that is dynamic and transformational. We believe that Christians don't simply gather to exchange doctrinal affirmations. Rather, believers are called by God to get into each other's lives. We are family, for better or for worse, and we need to connect with each other.

Community is not built through sitting in the same building and singing the same songs. It is forged in the fires of life. When we know each other deeply—the good, the bad, and the ugly—community is experienced. Community grows when we learn to rejoice with one another, celebrating life. Roots grow deep when we know we are loved by others and are free to extend love to them as well. Finally, community deepens and is built when we commit to serve each other and let others serve us. This process of doing ministry and humbly receiving the ministry of others is critical for healthy community life.

Build Community Through Knowing and Being Known

We all long to know others deeply and to be fully known by them. Although we might run from this level of intimacy at times, we all want to have people in our lives who trust us enough to disclose the deep and tender parts of themselves. In turn, we want to reveal some of our feelings, expressing them freely to people we trust.

The first section of each of these six sessions creates a place for deep knowing and being known. Through serious reflection on the truth of Scripture, you will be invited to communicate parts of your heart and life with your small group members. You might even discover yourself opening parts of your heart that you have normally kept hidden. The Bible study and discussion questions do not encourage surface conversation. The only way to go deep in knowing others and being known by them is to dig deep, and this takes some work. Knowing others also takes trust—that you will honor each other and respect each other's confidences.

Build Community Through Celebrating and Being Celebrated

If you have not had a good blush recently, read a short book in the Bible called Song of Songs. It's a record of a bride and groom writing poetic and romantic love letters to each other. They are freely celebrating every conceivable aspect of each other's personality, character, and physical appearance. At one point the groom says, "You have made my heart beat fast with a single glance from your eyes." Song of Songs is a reckless celebration of life, love, and all that is good.

We need to recapture the joy and freedom of celebration. In each session your group will commit to celebrate together. Although there are many ways to express joy, we will let our expression of celebration come through prayer. In each session you will take time to come before the God of joy and celebrate who He is and what He is doing. You will also have opportunity to celebrate what God is doing in your life and the lives of those who are a part of your small group. You will become a community of affirmation, celebration, and joy through your prayer time together.

You will need to be sensitive during this time of prayer together. Not everyone feels comfortable praying with a group of people. Be aware that each person is starting at a different place in their freedom to pray in a group, and be patient. Seek to promote a warm and welcoming atmosphere where each person can stretch a little and learn what it means to be a community that celebrates with God in the center.

Build Community Through Loving and Being Loved

Unless we are exchanging deeply committed levels of love with a few people, we will die slowly on the inside. This is precisely why so many people feel almost nothing at all. If we don't learn to exchange love with family and friends, we will eventually grow numb and no longer believe love is even a possibility. This is not God's plan. He hungers for us to be loved and to give love to others. As a matter of fact, He wants this for us even more than we want it for ourselves.

Every session in this study will address the area of loving and being loved. You will be challenged, in your personal life and as a small group, to be intentional and consistent about building love relationships. You will get practical tools and be encouraged to set measurable goals for giving and receiving love.

Build Community Through Serving and Being Served

Community is about serving and humbly allowing others to serve you. The single most stirring example of this is recorded in John 13, where Jesus takes the position of the lowest servant and washes the feet of His followers. He gives them a powerful example and then calls them to follow. Servanthood is at the very core of community. To sustain deep relationships over a long period of time, there must be humility and a willingness to serve each other.

At the close of each session will be a clear challenge to servanthood. As a group, and as individual followers of Christ, you will discover that community is built through serving others. You will also find that your own small group members will grow in their ability to extend service to your life.

Bible Study Basics

To get the most out of this study, you will need to prepare and participate. Here are some guidelines to help you.

Preparing for the Study

1. If possible, even if you are not the leader, look over each lesson before you meet, read the Bible passages, and answer the questions. The more you are prepared, the more you will gain from the study.
2. Begin your preparation time with prayer. Ask God to help you understand the passage and apply it to your life.
3. A good modern translation, such as the New International Version, the New American Standard Bible, or the New Revised Standard Version, will give you the most help. Questions in this guide are based on the New International Version.
4. Read and reread the passages. You must know what the passage says before you can understand what it means and how it applies to you.
5. Write your answers in the spaces provided in the study guide. This will help you to participate more fully in the discussion, and will also help you personalize what you are learning.
6. Keep a Bible dictionary handy to look up unfamiliar words, names, or places.

Participating in the Study

1. Be willing to join in the discussion. The leader of the group will not be lecturing but will encourage people to discuss what they have learned in the passage. Plan to share what God has taught you during your preparation time.
2. Stick to the passages being studied. Base your answers on the verses being discussed rather than on outside authorities such as commentaries or your favorite author or speaker.

3. Try to be sensitive to the other members of the group. Listen attentively when they speak, and be affirming whenever you can. This will encourage more hesitant members of the group to participate.
4. Be careful not to dominate the discussion. By all means participate, but allow others to have equal time.
5. If you are a discussion leader or a participant who wants further insights, you will find additional comments in the Leader's Notes at the back of this book.

Colossians—Discover the New You

There Is Hope!

When I was in college, a professor told me something very troubling. He told me there was little or no hope that people will change. As you might guess, this was a little discouraging for a young man who was planning on being a pastor.

The professor knew I was doing youth ministry and that I planned on starting a church. He affirmed my work with youth and was glad that our youth ministry had seen radical transformation in the lives of many young people. But he didn't want me to get my hopes too high. In an effort to brace me for the cold realities of church life, he told me that adults are set in their ways and just don't change.

I listened to his counsel and secretly prayed he was wrong. The scenario he painted gave me no hope, just the cold reality that I could spend a lifetime doing ministry in the local church and see no change, no transformation, no new life.

A couple of decades later I can say with joy and confidence, he was wrong! I have watched countless lives changed as people have become followers of Christ. People from every walk of life, from every age group, from every possible background, have experienced change beyond human explanation. God has the power to heal what is broken, bring joy to the depressed, give hope to the hopeless, and meaning to those who hunger to know what life is all about.

The book of Colossians is a signpost along the road of life saying, "If you want a whole new you, look no further than Jesus. There is hope!"

A Real Letter to a Real Church

When we read the words of Colossians, it is important to remember that these words are a letter written directly to a local church in the first century. Although the letter was not addressed to us in particular, it is still very valuable for the church today.

It is also helpful to remember that Paul had never visited the church at Colosse. He had planted many churches and spent a great deal of time encouraging them, but he was also glad and excited to encourage believers in congregations he had never visited.

Paul had started the church in Ephesus, and it became a very fruitful, growing, and healthy congregation. So, with time, some of the leaders from the church at Ephesus branched out and started a satellite church. This is how the church at Colosse began. It was a church plant out of the ministry of the church Paul planted and helped pastor in Ephesus. If we see Paul as a spiritual father to the church in Ephesus, this would make him a spiritual grandfather to the followers of Christ in Colosse. With this in mind, we can see why he cared so much for these people.

Paul learned of the great work happening in Colosse through reports he received from Epaphras and from others who had visited Colosse. Good rumors were floating around about this powerful new ministry. When Paul got the news of all God was doing at Colosse, he was in jail, locked up because of his ministry as a Christian pastor and church planter. Paul was in a minimum security jail in Rome. He was able to receive visitors freely and could correspond with the leaders from the churches he had started. It was at this time that Epaphras came to visit Paul in prison and amazed him with the report of all the great things happening in this new church plant in Colosse.

Epaphras reported that this new little congregation had launched into powerful and Christ-honoring ministry. The followers of Christ in Colosse were sold out for the gospel, were holding to their faith with tenacity, were telling others how to become followers of Christ, and were experiencing a powerful work of God. They were walking in faith, hope, and love!

Paul was receiving reports that lives were being changed, families were being healed, God was being honored, and more and more people were becoming fully devoted followers of Christ. In response to all of this, Paul wrote a powerful letter encouraging these people to keep on growing and changing in Christ-honoring ways.

If you long to experience newness in your life, this book of the Bible will point the way with clarity. If you want all of God's best in your home, workplace, church, and personal life, Colossians will teach you the pathway to a whole new you!

A New Look at the Church

COLOSSIANS 1:1–14

If ever there was a time in history when the ministry of the true church was sorely needed, it is now. Though church attendance dropped drastically in the decades following 1960, the rising surge of spiritual interest currently moving across the country suggests that many people are anguishing over spiritual emptiness.

Pollsters attribute much of this rising interest to growing disenchantment with the modern, materialistic lifestyle. In the secret places of their hearts, many people are concluding that there has to be more.

Another reason for the spiritual search is the increasing breakdown of relationships. Marriages are failing, families are fragmenting, and friendships are falling apart. As interpersonal trust levels sink to an all-time low, some people are beginning to look up. *Can God be trusted?* they wonder. *And can He somehow help me put my marriage, family, and friendships back together?*

People are waking up to the sobering reality that things are not as they should be, or as we long for them to be. With this awakening, many people are seeking for more. They are hungering for something that will truly satisfy. As people are searching for meaning, the church of Jesus Christ needs to rise up and let the world know that we have something to offer.

—Bill Hybels, *Rediscovering Church* (Zondervan, 1995)

Making the Connection

1. If you were born and raised in the church, what keeps you connected and part of your church community?

    It was the "right" thing to do. God expects you to be a part of the church

    If you were not raised in the church, what brought you into the life of the church, and what keeps you connected?

    A sense of family. People who know and care about one another.

    Becoming involved in other peoples lives...
    Sharing Life -

2. Take a moment and envision the ideal church. In your mind, what would have to be part of this church for it to be a biblically functioning community of believers?

    Dependence on the Scriptures for answers.
    Continually teaching from the Bible.
    Service to others -inside & outside the church
    Accept Gods Gift of Salvation & His
    Gift of Life w/ Joy

    What would not be part of this community of people?

    Changing principles (and rules) to meet today's society.

    All the problems we fall Back into when we Dont Allow God to rule our lives...

Knowing and Being Known

Read Colossians 1:1–8

3. In this passage the apostle Paul gives five trademarks of a biblically functioning community of Christ followers. What are these trademarks, and why is each one essential for a healthy church?

Trademark:	Why is it essential for a healthy church?
Faith ~~Praying~~	
Love	
Hope	Assurance of salvation
Truth	
Growth	

4. Paul begins by affirming the central and core pillar of any biblically functioning community: true faith in Jesus Christ (vv. 4–5). Why is unwavering faith in Jesus Christ on the top of the list when it comes to trademarks of a true church?

Requirement for salvation is faith in Christ

When you say "I believe in Jesus Christ," what does this mean to you?

Belief in his existance and that he paid the price for our sins,

What Is the Church?

Throughout history many people have tried to answer the question, What is the church? Here are a few efforts to give a concise answer to a seemingly complex question:

To speak of the church as anything other than "the living congregation of the living Lord Jesus" is to miss the whole point and to become meaningless in our understanding of what the church is.

—Karl Barth

The church is God's agent on earth ... the medium through which He expresses Himself to the world. God has no other redeeming agency on the earth.

—Melvin Hodges

I believe that the Son of God through his Spirit and Word, out of the entire human race, from the beginning of the world to its end, gathers, protects, and preserves for himself a community chosen for eternal life and united in true faith. And of this community I am and always will be a living member.

—The Heidelberg Catechism

5. What message do we send to seekers when the members of a local congregation really love each other (vv. 4–5)?

Seekers discover a warm & caring atmosphere

What message do we send to God?

Obedience to his commandments.

What is one practical and tangible way your small group members can show love to each other?

Pray, emotional support & physically helping

6. Paul lifts up Epaphras as an example of a "faithful minister of Christ." This is a person whose life and faith has impacted the lives of other Christ followers in a positive way. Who has been an Epaphras in your life?

Sonya

How has their faith and love for Jesus impacted your life as a Christ follower?

Encourages me to do more for others without repayment or without being asked.

Read Colossians 1:9–14

7. What did Paul pray for the followers of Christ in Colosse?

For God to give them knowledge of His will.

Praying When Things Are Going Great!

Paul continues the thanksgiving section (1:3–23) by informing the Colossians how he and Timothy had specifically interceded for them in prayer. The initial success of the gospel in Colosse does not lull them into slackening their prayer efforts for the Colossians. *Quite the reverse, it leads to even more intense prayer.* They have continued to pray for them because of what God has already done for them and because of their faith and love. By sharing this petition on their behalf, Paul reacquaints them with their blessings, their obligations, and their potential in Christ.

—David E. Garland, *The NIV Application Commentary Series, Colossians/Philemon* (Zondervan, 1998)

What is one part of Paul's prayer that jumps out at you and seems fresh and new?

"So that you may have great endurance and patience"

8. How can this prayer be used as a model to give direction as you pray for *one* of these groups:

    • For your small group members
    • For your church
    • For other churches in your community
    • For the church around the world

9. What are ways we can grow in our knowledge of God's will for our lives and the life of the church (v. 9)?

Pray for wisdom & knowledge

Describe a time when you had a clear sense of God giving you knowledge of His will for your life.

10. What is one area of your life where you need God's strength and power right now (v. 11)?

Work

How can your small group members be agents of God's strength as you face this situation?

Pray for Bill & I. We need to focus on the positive things that are happening.

11. How have you experienced the transfer of your life "from the dominion of darkness" to a new place in Christ's kingdom (vv. 13–14)?

God has slowly changed my priorities as I have grown closer to him.

Describe one life attitude or action that has changed since you have made this relocation.

I try to put ~~family~~ activities with family and friends ahead of household tasks. (Less emphasis on what I need to get done.)

Celebrating and Being Celebrated

Take a few moments to make an inheritance assessment. Paul is clear that we have a whole new inheritance once we become children of God (v. 12). Brainstorm as a group and list many of the promises and possessions you have in your inheritance from God, your heavenly Father.

Our inheritance includes:

Eternal life
Support in times of trouble

Pray together and lift up your voices in praise and celebration for the inheritance you have in Jesus Christ.

Loving and Being Loved

Over the centuries God has worked through His church to touch countless lives. The local church is the hope of the world and God's agent for transformation. In every generation God calls out leaders for the church who faithfully invest their lives in the local church. Many of these leaders have greatly influenced our lives, but we have never told them. Commit as a group to write letters to previous pastors who are retired, or to those who have served your church in the past and now serve other congregations. Express your love to them and thank them for investing their lives in the local church.

Serving and Being Served

There are few acts of service more powerful than consistent, intentional, faithful prayer for others. Commit as a group to pray for two churches each time you meet. First, commit to pray for the people in your church. Use Paul's outline from this passage, and pray for them to:

- Grow in their knowledge of God's will.
- Live a life worthy of the Lord.
- Be strengthened with God's power.
- Learn to celebrate their great inheritance in Christ.

Second, agree to pray for another group of Christians in your community. Identify a church that is seeking to honor Christ and become a biblically functioning community. Pray for them each time you meet. At the end of this time, have a group representative volunteer to contact the church and let the pastor know that you have been praying for them. Be specific and let the pastor and church leaders know that you have been praying Colossians 1:9–14 for them. This can be done through a letter, phone call, e-mail, or even a personal visit.

A New Look at Jesus

COLOSSIANS 1:15–27

We need to put first things first!

We live in a day of pathological busyness. For many people, a hurried and full schedule is a badge of their own self-worth. Even followers of Christ can find themselves doing all sorts of things for God as their schedules get more and more congested. Sadly, in our pursuit of "doing" for God, we can forget the very One we are serving. In our busy and driven lives, Jesus can get pushed off to the side while other things take center stage. This was the very reality that the apostle John addressed in the book of Revelation:

> *I know your deeds, your hard work and your perseverance.*
> *I know that you cannot tolerate wicked men, that you have*
> *tested those who claim to be apostles but are not, and have*
> *found them false. You have persevered and have endured*
> *hardships for my name, and have not grown weary.*
> *Yet I hold this against you: You have forsaken your first*
> *love. Remember the height from which you have fallen!*
> *Repent and do the things you did at first.*
>
> (Revelation 2:2–5)

Notice that these followers of Christ were doing many things right. They were working hard, standing strong during a time of persecution, holding to the truth, and confronting what was false. These were people who were heavily invested in the things of God. Yet something was very wrong. In the midst of all they were doing for God, they had lost their first love.

Making the Connection

1. Tell about a time in your life when you had a deep sense of God's closeness and felt Christ was first in your heart and life.

   What helped create this sense of closeness and connectedness to Jesus?

Knowing and Being Known

Read Colossians 1:15–20

2. The apostle Paul paints a vivid and detailed picture of Jesus Christ in this passage. What do you learn about Jesus from looking at this portrait?

At the Center of It All

At the center of the Christian faith lies a picture. Christian art and architecture, literature and hymns, are dominated by the symbol of the cross. A symbol, however, both invites and demands thought and reflection. What are we to make of this symbol? What does it tell us about God and the world, or about our nature and ultimate destiny? Why is it that at the center of a faith in a loving God lies a symbol of death and despair—the dreadful picture of a man dying through crucifixion?

The cross is . . . a powerful challenge to the complacency of the Christian church. The cross continually raises questions for the church, which dares to call itself "Christian" after the one who was crucified and rose again, and yet seems to prefer to look for the grounds of its identity and relevance elsewhere than in the crucified Christ.

—Alister E. McGrath, *The Mystery of the Cross* (Zondervan, 1988)

3. In these six short verses, we see Jesus as the eternal God. As Jesus Himself says in Revelation 1:8, "I am the Alpha and the Omega . . . who is, and who was, and who is to come, the Almighty." According to this passage, respond to *one* of these questions:

What *has* Jesus done?

What *is* Jesus doing now?

What *will* Jesus do in the future?

4. Jesus is the One who holds everything together (v. 17). How have you seen Him function as the cosmic adhesive that holds your life together?

5. Jesus is the head of the church (v. 18). What do you think Jesus would say to *one* of these people or groups:

    • To the wealthy church member who threatens to stop giving if he does not get his way
    • To a church board that believes it is in charge of the church
    • To a congregation that honors their pastor more than Christ
    • To a pastor who demands unquestioning allegiance

Why is it essential for Jesus to always be on the throne of the church?

6. The divinity (godhead) and death of Jesus are inseparable (1:19–20). How have you experienced peace in your life through the death of Jesus Christ on the cross?

Read Colossians 1:21–23

7. By using the words *once*, pointing to the past, and *but now* pointing to the present, Paul offers "before" and "after" snapshots of our lives (vv. 21–22). What does Paul say about our lives before we become followers of Christ?

What does Paul say about our lives after we become Christ followers?

A Powerful Reminder

The early Christians delighted to speak of the great change brought about for them by the gospel. The contrast between what "once we were" and what "now by grace we are" was frequently on their lips in testimony. Here, however, we are not listening to a Colossian Christian testifying to Paul, but to Paul testifying to the Colossians about what happened to them ... the apostle thinks it wise to remind them what great things Christ had done for them.

Of course he does this in order to provide for them an illustration, drawn from their own undeniable experience, of the truth of reconciliation. What he has been expounding is no unproven theory, but truth they have been able to verify in life.

—R. C. Lucas, *Fullness & Freedom* (InterVarsity, 1980)

8. If people could see a video-log of your life before you were a fully devoted follower of Christ, what would surprise them?

9. Paul presents those outside of faith as "alienated from God," "enemies" of God, and filled with "evil behavior" (v. 21). Why is Paul so strong in his language when he speaks of those who don't have faith in Jesus Christ?

10. Paul presents followers of Christ in a whole different light, "holy," "without blemish," and "free from accusation" (v. 22). How do these affirmations make you feel?

11. How do these "before" and "after" snapshots challenge you to be more intentional about making Christ known to those who are still seeking?

Who is one seeker you are praying will enter a relationship with Jesus, and how can your small group members pray for you in this relationship?

Celebrating and Being Celebrated

Jesus Christ is the same yesterday, today, and forever! He is the cosmic adhesive that holds the entire universe together. He was eternally before us, preparing the way. He is with us every moment. And He is already in heaven preparing a place for us, an eternal home beyond our wildest imagination.

Take time to pray as a group and lift up praise for the work of Jesus Christ. Pray in three directions:

- Jesus, we praise you for all you have done in the past for us. . . .
- We praise you for what you are doing to sustain, guide, and reveal your love to us today. . . .
- And we celebrate what lies ahead, all that you have planned for us tomorrow and for eternity. . . .

Loving and Being Loved

Paul is emphatic that followers of Christ are headed for a joy-filled eternity with God. At the same time, he honestly portrays those who are not followers of Christ as alienated from God and headed for a Christless eternity. These people are lost.

We need to live with a deep conviction that lost people matter to God and they should matter to us. The greatest act of love is to help others come to know God's love and the transformation they can experience through a relationship with Jesus Christ.

Take time as a group to make a list of people you love and care about who do not have a relationship with Jesus Christ:

Kirt's Brother — Chris

Deb's Brother — Mark

Steve's Friend — Red Knouff

Bill's Brother & Sister

Jerry's Brother — Ron

Commit to pray for the people on this list and to encourage your group members to continue seeking opportunities to show the love of Jesus to these people. Also, be sure to report to your group members when you see God moving in the life of a person on this list. You might also consider planning a social event for your group, and invite people on this list to attend.

Serving and Being Served

Service in the name of Jesus Christ is not always easy or fun. Sometimes there is a price to pay. Service cost Jesus His life, and He invites us to take up the cross and follow Him (Luke 9:23–24). The apostle Paul was deeply aware of the cost involved with serving others in the name of Jesus:

> *Now I rejoice in what was suffered for you, and I fill up in my flesh what is still lacking in regard to Christ's afflictions, for the sake of his body, which is the church. I have become its servant by the commission God gave me to present to you the word of God in its fullness—the mystery that has been kept hidden for ages and generations, but is now disclosed to the saints. To them God has chosen to make known among the Gentiles the glorious riches of this mystery, which is Christ in you, the hope of glory.*
>
> (Colossians 1:24–27)

The hope we have in Christ is a message that needs to be brought to all people. This is rarely done without an investment of time, energy, money, or even personal suffering. Talk as a group about some way you can further the cause of Christ and bring the message of Christ to others. Commit together to count the cost and invest your time, energy, money, or whatever it takes to meet this Christ-honoring goal.

A New Foundation

COLOSSIANS 1:28–2:23

We have all heard the story of the three little pigs. All of them lived with the threat of the big bad wolf coming by some day and gobbling them up. In an effort to prepare for this coming danger, they each built a house. One of the pigs was fairly unmotivated, so he threw up a hut made of straw. Another of the pigs built his house out of sticks. The third took the time and had the foresight to build his house out of bricks.

When the big bad wolf came to the first pig's house, he huffed, puffed, and quickly blew the straw house down. This was also the end result of the wolf's huffing and puffing at the second house—the stick house blew to pieces. However, at the third pig's house, no amount of huffing, puffing, or blowing made any difference. The structure was safe and secure.

This led to one content piggy, and a winded and frustrated wolf!

Among other possible morals of the story, is this . . . our building materials really do matter. Jesus gave a warning for all people to be sure that the house of their life was built on a safe, sound, and secure foundation. If the foundation was weak, even the strongest house would come crashing down. Jesus put it this way:

Therefore everyone who hears these words of mine and puts them into practice is like a wise man who built his house on the rock. The rain came down, the streams rose, and the winds blew and beat against that house; yet it did not fall, because it had its foundation on the rock. But everyone who hears these words of mine and does not put them into practice is like a foolish man who built his house on sand. The rain came down, the streams rose, and the winds blew and beat against that house, and it fell with a great crash.

(Matthew 7:24–27)

Making the Connection

1. What are some of the foundations on which people try to build their lives?

Stuff: —

Family ...

What can happen to people when they seek to build their house on shifting sand?

Knowing and Being Known

Read Colossians 1:28–2:7

2. What do you learn about the passion and heart of the apostle Paul toward those who were young in their faith (1:28–2:1)?

Jesus Christ ... The Beginning and the End

The true Church *holds fast to the faith which it has received*. It never forgets the teaching about Christ which it has been taught. This does not mean a frozen orthodoxy in which all adventure of thought is heresy. We have only to remember how in Colossians Paul strikes out new lines in his thinking about Jesus Christ to see how far that was from his intention. But it does mean that there are certain beliefs which do remain the foundation and do not change. Paul might travel down new pathways of thought but he always began and ended with the unchanging and unchangeable truth that Jesus Christ is Lord.

—William Barclay, *The Letter to the Colossians, The Daily Study Bible Series*
(Westminster Press, 1957)

How can his example influence the way you relate to those who are new followers of Christ?

3. Paul is clear that the only lasting and stable foundation for life is Jesus Christ. What do you learn about Jesus Christ as the foundation for your life from this passage (2:2–7)?

Beware! Thin Ice!

We all appreciate signs that warn us about potential danger.

BEWARE! THIN ICE! A pond in the winter can be a great place to ice skate or fish, unless the ice is too thin. A fun afternoon outdoors can turn into an instant tragedy. However, a well-placed signpost can warn people of the potential danger and save them from disaster.

BEWARE OF DOG! The very words create images of Doberman pinschers, pit bulls, and Rottweilers. Just the potential of coming face-to-face with a growling, barking, angry guard dog will keep people away.

BRIDGE OUT AHEAD! Slow down! Hit the brakes! No one keeps racing ahead when they read a sign with these words.

Let's admit it, if there is potential danger ahead, we want to know about it and be forewarned so we can avoid the trouble.

4. Paul uses three images to describe the importance of our lives being connected with our Savior. How does each image help you see a different aspect of your connectedness to Jesus?

   • An agricultural image: Be *"rooted"* in your faith in Jesus.
   • A construction image: Be *"built up"* in your faith in Jesus.
   • An exercise (athletic) image: Be *"strengthened"* in your faith in Jesus.

5. Imagine yourself sitting down for a conversation face-to-face with Jesus. How would you finish this statement to demonstrate that you are "overflowing with thankfulness" (2:7)?

   Jesus, I thank you for . . .

Read Colossians 2:8–15

6. Read Colossians 2:8 as if it is a warning sign posted with bold letters for every follower of Christ to see. What is the content and purpose of this warning sign?

> See to it that no one takes you captive through hollow and deceptive philosophy, which depends on human tradition and the basic principles of this world rather than on Christ.

7. What are some of the "deceptive philosophies," "human traditions," and "principles of this world" that have power to take people captive?

What is one "philosophy," "tradition," or "principle" that had you captive, but Jesus Christ has set you free from its power?

8. Paul presents Jesus Christ as the only key that can unlock the prison doors and set captives free from the philosophies, traditions, and principles of this world. What is Paul's message for those who are still held captive by the philosophies of this world?

Set Free from Religious Chains

We may not be absolutely certain about what "philosophy" Paul was attacking in the letter to the Colossians, but the text does provide warnings against any "religious" or secular phenomena with similar features that may resurface in our setting. . . . We should be on our guard against any religious practice or worldview that promotes any or all of the following things:

- Anything that judges and disqualifies others according to arbitrary human measures.
- Anything that substitutes sham battles with asceticism for the real battle with sin, which Christ has already won for us.
- Anything that makes subjective feelings or mystic states the norm over the historical event of Christ's crucifixion and resurrection.
- Anything that places more importance on divine intermediaries, such as angels, than on the divine reality of Christ.
- Anything that cuts people off from Christ, the Head, or Christ's people, the body.

—David E. Garland, *NIV Application Commentary, Colossians/Philemon*
(Zondervan, 1998)

Read Colossians 2:16–23

9. Paul calls us to build our lives on the foundation of Christ. He has warned us about the shaky foundation of worldly philosophies. Now he hits even closer to home. What does Paul warn us about the danger of trying to build our lives on the foundation of being "religious"?

What is the difference between being "religious" and being a follower of Christ?

10. What are some of the religious practices or traditions that can give people a false sense of security?

How does building your life on the foundation of Jesus Christ bring a freedom and joy that no religious system could ever offer?

Celebrating and Being Celebrated

In Matthew 7:24–27, Jesus speaks of the "rains," "streams," and "winds" of this life. He promises that those who build their lives on Him as a foundation will stand strong during the storms. Take time as a group to pray together and celebrate the way God has sustained you and protected you during the tough times you have faced.

Loving and Being Loved

As followers of Christ we know that our lives are built on the firm foundation of a love relationship with Jesus. However, we can get caught up in religious traditions and legalisms. Sometimes doing good things can become more important than living in a close relationship with Jesus. This is exactly what happened in the church of Ephesus in the first century. Jesus spoke to these believers and said:

> I know your deeds, your hard work and your perseverance. I know that you cannot tolerate wicked men, that you have tested those who claim to be apostles but are not, and have found them false. You have persevered and have endured hardships for my name, and have not grown weary.
> Yet I hold this against you: You have forsaken your first love. Remember the height from which you have fallen! Repent and do the things you did at first.
>
> (Revelation 2:2–5)

Invite your small group members to challenge you to put Jesus Christ first in your life. Seek to create a place where each group member feels free to ask the others if Jesus Christ is first in their heart, life, and schedule.

Serving and Being Served

In this session we are reminded of the apostle Paul's deep and passionate concern for new believers (1:28–2:1). Paul was ready to do whatever it took to encourage, support, and challenge these people to become fully devoted followers of Christ.

Talk as a group and identify two new believers in your congregation. Commit as a group to do three things in the coming month:

1. Pray regularly for these two people to grow strong in their faith.
2. Call both people and let them know you are praying for them. Also, give them verbal affirmation of their new faith and tell them of the joy you have experienced as a Christ follower.
3. Look for opportunities to connect these new believers with mature followers of Christ. You might even want to invite them to some social gathering you have for your small group members.

A Whole New You

COLOSSIANS 3:1–17

Let's just be honest and admit it, we care a great deal about what others think and say about us. This reality drives so much of what we do. It also has a powerful impact on how we see ourselves. We can try to fight it, but there is something in each of us that cares deeply about how others see us.

With all of this in mind, answer this question: Whose opinion, thoughts, and words about you matter the most?

Our answer should be . . . God! No one else's thoughts, feelings, or words should matter nearly as much as God's.

In the first two chapters of Colossians, we get to listen in on what God has to say about followers of Christ. In these chapters we discover exactly how God sees us. In a few specific verses, we get a heavenly perspective on our position as Christ followers, and it's amazing! As you read these passages, notice what has already been accomplished on our behalf because of Christ.

> *For he has rescued us from the dominion of darkness and brought us into the kingdom of the Son he loves, in whom we have redemption, the forgiveness of sins.*
>
> (Colossians 1:13–14)

> *For God was pleased to have all his fullness dwell in him, and through him to reconcile to himself all things, whether things on earth or things in heaven, by making peace through his blood, shed on the cross. Once you were alienated from God and were enemies in your minds because of your evil behavior. But now he has reconciled you by Christ's physical body through death to present you holy in his sight, without blemish and free from accusation.*
>
> (Colossians 1:19–22)

You have been given fullness in Christ, who is the head over every power and authority.

(Colossians 2:10)

When you were dead in your sins and in the uncircumcision of your sinful nature, God made you alive with Christ. He forgave us all our sins, having canceled the written code, with its regulations, that was against us and that stood opposed to us; he took it away, nailing it to the cross.

(Colossians 2:13–14)

Do you sense the finality of what God is declaring? Believers have their position secure. We need to stop listening to what everyone else says about us, and start listening to what God says. His opinion should matter more than what anyone else thinks or says. He has gone on record. Believe it!

Making the Connection

1. Who is one person in your life whose opinion has always mattered a great deal to you? Why did this person's opinion matter so much?

2. If God's opinion mattered to you more than anyone else's, how would you view yourself, and other Christ followers, after reading the first two chapters of Colossians?

Knowing and Being Known

Read Colossians 3:1–4

3. Because of our new position in Christ, we are called to a new mind-set and heart condition. How do our thought processes change when we become Christ followers?

   How does the condition of our hearts change when we enter a living relationship with Jesus?

4. What is one aspect of your heart condition or mind-set that has changed dramatically since becoming a Christian?

Lust Is Lurking

I think of a gentleman I met several years ago—a fine itinerant Bible teacher. He said he had been keeping a confidential list of men who were once outstanding expositors of the Scripture, capable and respected men of God . . . who have shipwrecked their faith on the shoals of moral defilement. During the previous week, he said, he had entered the name of number forty-two in his book. . . .

A chill ran down my spine when he told me that story. No one is immune. You're not. I'm not. Lust is no respecter of persons. . . . Its alluring voice can infiltrate the most intelligent mind and cause its victim to believe its lies and respond to its appeal. And beware—it never gives up. . . . It never runs out of ideas. Bolt the front door and it'll rattle at the bedroom window, crawl into the living room through the TV screen, or wink at you out of a magazine in the den. . . .

—Charles Swindoll, *Come Before Winter* (Multnomah Press, 1985)

Read Colossians 3:5–9

5. In this passage Paul uses the image of stripping off old dirty clothes (sinful actions). What are these actions that we need to get rid of, and how can they be damaging to our lives as followers of Christ if we don't strip them off?

6. The first three examples Paul uses deal with sexual sin. Why do you think Paul attacks this area of temptation first and with such ferocity?

What are some of the sources of sexual temptation that we need to learn to avoid if we are going to keep our lives pure?

7. Another clear area of warning is how we use our words (3:8–9). What is the danger of each of these sins of the mouth:

   • Slander

   • Filthy Language

   • Lying

What is one strategy you have found for stripping away the power of one of these areas of verbal sin?

A Whole New World

Paul is calling upon his readers to have done with their old life-style and its habits, inclinations, and goals and to live as those who, at the beginning of their new life in Christ, entered a new world as members of a new humanity which is alive unto God. Nor should we forget that, while Paul may well be utilizing traditional forms of (catechetical-teaching) expression which were common in the early churches, there would be special relevance of this teaching to the men and women at Colossae who were puzzled over rival directions for the Christian way of life offered in the name of false teachers in their midst. Paul's answer and antidote is a simple declaration of the Lordship of Christ and what it means to live under that rule. His readers (he reminds them) were those who professed allegiance to the Lord Christ in conversion and renewal. Let them now act out that profession in pursuing ethical ideals whose pattern is set by their life in . . . Christ Jesus.

—Ralph P. Martin, *Colossians, New Century Bible* (Oliphants, 1974)

Read Colossians 3:10–17

8. Again Paul uses the image of clothing. This time he gives more than ten examples of the new behaviors that Christ followers should wear like a garment. What are these new attitudes and actions, and why must they be in the wardrobe of a fully devoted follower of Christ?

9. What are you doing in your life to more consistently wear *one* of these garments?

10. What is one of these garments that you have a hard time wearing, and how can your small group members help you in your effort to "clothe yourself" with this attitude or behavior?

Celebrating and Being Celebrated

One of the best ways to battle the temptation of sin is to keep our minds on what is good and pure. "Whatever is true, whatever is noble, whatever is right, whatever is pure, whatever is lovely, whatever is admirable—if anything is excellent or praiseworthy—think about such things" (Philippians 4:8). Take time as a group to pray together and celebrate those things that are right, pure, and praiseworthy. Rejoice in such things as Christ's work in you, Christ-honoring relationships, gifts of the Spirit, fruit of the Spirit, freedom in Christ—the list goes on and on.

Loving and Being Loved

When two people are very close friends, sometimes they share clothes. Use this image as you consider how you can support and love other members of your small group. If you have a piece of "clothing" (a developed and Christ-honoring characteristic) another small group member would like to develop, seek creative ways to share this with them. Can you spend time together in a context where they can watch you exercise compassion, kindness, or gentleness? Can you tell them stories about how God developed this character trait in your life? Can you encourage them and pray for them as they seek to develop this characteristic in their own life? If two members of your group agree to do their best to share "clothes" in this way, be sure to report back to your group when you see growth and maturity because of this experience.

Serving and Being Served

Most of the "Serving and Being Served" ideas over the past sessions have been corporate in nature. This one might be something you can address with your whole group, but you may want to make this a one-on-one accountability project with a specific person (most likely same gender) in your small group.

Allow one of your small group members to serve you by asking him or her to pray for you and keep you accountable to seek sexual purity by guarding your mind from unhealthy images and input. If you struggle with sexual temptation or lust because of a stream of unhealthy material you allow into your mind, confess this to God, and to a brother or sister in your small group. Let them know the point of your struggle and ask them to check in with you occasionally to see if you are shutting the door on this unhealthy input. Pray faithfully for each other and challenge each other to live with purity in this area of your life.

A New Look at Relationships

COLOSSIANS 3:18–4:1

I used to live with a real naivete when it came to human relationships. I believed I could look at a couple or family in church and determine the condition of their spiritual life. They seemed so mature. They looked so good. Every outward indication was that they were fully devoted followers of Christ with rock-solid faith and a life to match.

Yet, with time, I would hear of certain church members' behavior in their homes, and I discovered they had a lot of inconsistencies between what they declared in church and how they treated their family members. They listened to the sermon, nodded their head in agreement, smiled, went home, and seemed to disregard all they had heard. As a pastor I was shocked and hurt at this apparent hypocrisy.

Then I would hear of people in leadership in the church who were conducting themselves in a way that dishonored Christ in the marketplace. They would volunteer many hours to serve in a specific ministry area, but their business practices were questionable. They appeared to have integrity and authenticity in their relationships with church members, but their coworkers knew a whole different person. Again I found myself angry, frustrated, and shocked that they could live with such discontinuity between their faith and their behavior in the workplace.

I was disappointed, hurt, and amazed by these dramatic inconsistencies. *Then I looked in the mirror.* I recognized the battle that rages inside of me. I still struggle to live my faith with consistency and integrity. I had to admit that, as a fully devoted follower of Christ, I am still learning how to honor Christ in my family and work relationships.

In the home and in the workplace, people see us as we are. We can fake it for an hour a week at church, but no one can keep up a facade for forty to fifty hours each week! In our homes and in the workplace, people know who we really are . . . for better or for worse.

Making the Connection

1. If one of your family members could tell your small group one thing about you that would surprise them, what would it be?

2. What is one adjective your coworkers would use to describe you and your work habits, and why would they use this descriptive word?

Knowing and Being Known

Read Colossians 3:18–21

3. Put Paul's challenge to each family member *in your own words*. You can use one word, or a whole sentence, but keep it brief and direct:

Wives (v. 18)—

Husbands (v. 19)—

Children (v. 20)—

Fathers (parents) (v. 21)—

The Acid Test

We can show up at church and look right, act right, talk right, and give right. But our home might be a war zone. The drive over to church can be filled with cutting words and shouting matches, or with ice-cold silence. But once we walk into the church building, it is easy to put on a performance worthy of an Oscar. Almost anyone can fake it for an hour and a half. And some of us have become masters at maintaining the illusion.

We can sit next to our spouse, smile at our children, and play the role of "happy family." But the acid test comes inside the walls of our homes. Our Christian faith is not expressed in one or two performances a week in public as a family. Followers of Christ know that real faith brings real change in the relationships of those who are closest to us . . . our family members.

Of all the challenges God could have spoken to each of these groups of people, why do you think He chose to emphasize these specific ones?

4. Imagine countless homes where each member of the family willingly and joyfully followed Paul's counsel in these verses. How would this impact *one* of these areas:

   • Marriage relationships
   • Parent-child relationships
   • The local church
   • Society at large
   • Seekers

5. Imagine countless homes filled with husbands, wives, dads, moms, and kids who claim to be Christ followers, but who disregard how their faith should impact family relationships. How will this neglectful attitude affect *one* of these areas:

   • Marriage relationships
   • Parent-child relationships
   • The local church
   • Society at large
   • Seekers

6. If you are married, what is one goal you want to set for developing and deepening your relationship with your spouse? If you are single, what goal can you set for growing a relationship with a family member, friend, or coworker?

How can your small group members pray for you and support you as you seek to reach this goal?

7. What is one goal you want to set for developing and deepening your relationship with a child or parent?

How can your small group members pray for you and support you as you seek to reach this goal?

A New Job for a New Person

Paul is addressing the relationship of slaves and masters. It is important that we remember, by some estimations, that over half of the Roman world was in some kind of slavery in the first century. Paul's words are not written to affirm slavery or advocate the continuation of this godless institution. Paul is actually seeking to give dignity to those who are slaves and a challenge to those who were masters.

Although we can't draw a one-to-one parallel, there are transferable principles between slavery and modern-day vocational life. The words to slaves can speak volumes to employees, and the words to masters can be of great benefit to employers. In these few verses we will find a deep challenge to how our faith can impact our vocational life.

Read Colossians 3:22–4:1

8. What is Paul's counsel for employees (slaves) in the workplace?

   What would happen in your workplace if everyone followed Paul's vocational guidelines?

9. What is Paul's counsel for employers (masters) toward their employees?

What would happen in your workplace if managers and employers followed Paul's guidelines?

10. What can you do to live out the principles for the workplace drawn from this passage?

How can your small group members keep you accountable to implement these actions in your workplace?

Celebrating and Being Celebrated

Work is a gift from God! We don't always see it this way, but God does. All we have to do is read the opening chapters of Genesis to discover the goodness of work. In the garden, before the fall, in perfect paradise, God gives meaningful work to Adam.

The LORD God took the man and put him in the Garden of Eden to work it and take care of it.

(Genesis 2:15)

Take time as a group to pray together and thank God for the work He has given you. From the marketplace to working in the home, all work is a gift from God. Celebrate His provision of meaningful work.

Loving and Being Loved

Plan a small group gathering that includes your family members. Invite children, parents, and maybe even siblings. Make this event fun and unstructured (maybe a picnic, barbecue, or party of some kind). You will learn a great deal about each other as you get to know family members better.

At some point at this event, gather the whole group together and do two things:

1. Give your group members a chance to articulate their love and appreciation for their family . . . publicly!
2. Have a member of your small group offer a prayer of thanksgiving for all that these families members mean to each other.

Serving and Being Served

Talk as a group and identify a specific need that one of your family members has. It might be a parent, grandparent, or child. Talk as a group about how you can meet this need. Commit together to serve this person in the coming month. Let this be a starting point for inviting each other into the life of your family.

....A New Voice

COLOSSIANS 4:2–18

Words have power!

There are several exhortations in Scripture that remind us of the awesome power we have every time we speak. Our voice can do great good or great harm, depending on how we use it. In the Old Testament book of Proverbs, we are given some very sobering reminders of just how powerful our voices can be:

> *Reckless words pierce like a sword, but the tongue of the wise brings healing.*
>
> (Proverbs 12:18)

> *The tongue has the power of life and death, and those who love it will eat its fruit.*
>
> (Proverbs 18:21)

In the New Testament, James takes up this same theme and warns followers of Christ to be very careful how they use their words. James wakes us up with these words:

> *When we put bits into the mouths of horses to make them obey us, we can turn the whole animal. Or take ships as an example. Although they are so large and are driven by strong winds, they are steered by a very small rudder wherever the pilot wants to go. Likewise the tongue is a small part of the body, but it makes great boasts. Consider what a great forest is set on fire by a small spark. The tongue also is a fire, a world of evil among the parts of the body. It corrupts the whole person, sets the whole course of his life on fire, and is itself set on fire by hell.*
>
> (James 3:3–6)

From the beginning to the end of the Bible, God seeks to heighten our awareness of the power of our words. What we say to God in prayer really matters. The way we speak to seekers has a powerful impact on how they see Jesus. Our words to other followers of Christ can build them up or do great damage. It is time for followers of Christ to be sure our words and our voices reflect what is honoring to Christ in all of our relationships.

Making the Connection

1. How have you experienced the power of words to do harm and damage?

    Yes... we need to forgive & move on—

    How have you experienced encouragement or healing through words that were Christ-honoring?

    Many times —
    Stoke patud - S.E.

Knowing and Being Known

Read Colossians 4:2–4

2. What are some of the different kinds of prayer Paul mentions in this passage?

> 1. Opportunies to preach bospel
> 2. Pray for right speech

What are some different ways you can pray that are not mentioned in this passage?

> Psalm 51
> Confession 22
> Lauds 92
> praise

3. Paul invites the Colossians to pray for the mission of the church, proclaiming the message of Christ to those who don't know Him. Why is prayer for the mission of the church so critical?

> How Word will Be spread
> pray for those who are
> Doing it —

How can you pray for each other as you seek to bring the message of Christ to your neighborhoods, workplaces, families, and social settings?

> By getting sperling
> time getting to
> Know each other

60

An Unnatural, Natural Activity

Prayer is an unnatural activity.

From birth we have been learning the rules of self-reliance as we strain and struggle to achieve self-sufficiency. Prayer flies in the face of those deep-seated values. It is an assault on human autonomy, an indictment of independent living. To people in the fast lane, determined to make it on their own, prayer is an embarrassing interruption.

Prayer is alien to our proud human nature. And yet somewhere, someplace, probably all of us reach the point of falling to our knees, bowing our heads, fixing our attention on God and praying.

—Bill Hybels, *Too Busy Not to Pray* (InterVarsity, 1988)

Few activities are more unnatural than praying, and few are more natural. We resist relying on God, we fight the call to humble ourselves, and prayer is sometimes seen as a weak person's retreat from the real world. Yet when we begin to pray, when we meet God face-to-face, when we enter deeply into His presence, we discover our true home. Those who learn to drink deeply at the fountain of prayer find refreshment beyond compare. When we truly encounter God in prayer, we discover nothing is more natural—because we were made to be in relationship with Him!

4. Why is spontaneous, Spirit-led prayer that punctuates our day so important for followers of Christ?

> He would like us to Acknowledge his involvement in All the Affairs of our life

Why is it helpful for Christ followers to have a disciplined time and place to seek God in prayer on a regular basis?

> Forces us to focus

Signs of Maturity

We all want to see ourselves as mature followers of Christ. Here are a few questions we can ask ourselves on a regular basis that might help us make a personal assessment of how we are maturing in our faith:

- Do I have a deep desire, on a regular basis, to worship Christ?
- Do I have a hunger and thirst for the Word of God?
- Do I desire to be obedient in every area of my life?
- Do I have a strong desire for personal purity?
- Do I have a burden for those who are lost?

The final question in this list is not last because it is least important, but because it grows out of the previous four questions. When we are growing as worshipers, feeding on God's truth, obedient to God's leading, and deepening in personal purity, our hearts begin to change. We begin to realize that people matter to God, and they should matter to us. When we meet a person who is far from God, our hearts break, and we want to do whatever we can to help this person enter a life-changing relationship with Jesus.

How are you seeking to develop this practice in your own spiritual life?

Well...
Not much...
Thinking about it ✓

Read Colossians 4:5–6

5. If the apostle Paul was sitting in your small group right now, what counsel would he give you about how you should relate to those who are not followers of Christ?

6. Finish *one* of these statements as it relates to your relationship with a seeker:

   - One way I am seeking to be wise in my actions toward this person is . . .
   - One opportunity I am trying to make the most of is . . .
   - One way I am seeking to create thirst (interest) toward spiritual things is . . .
   - One way I am seeking to develop my ability to explain and defend my faith is . . .

7. Owners of bars have discovered that giving customers free chips, pretzels, or peanuts actually makes them money. The salt content in these "appetizers" creates thirst, and the customer buys more drinks. What have you discovered that you can sprinkle into your conversations with seekers that creates a thirst and interest in spiritual things?

Read Colossians 4:7–18

8. Who is one of the people in this portrait that stands out to you?

A Family Portrait

The apostle Paul was a team player. When he went on a mission trip, he always brought someone with him. When we read the account of Paul's travels, we discover that Barnabas, Silas, John Mark, and others accompanied him as partners in ministry. Paul realized that the work of God demanded participation. When God gives a vision, it takes people to carry it out. These people who worked with Paul in ministry became like a family to him.

We have all seen family portraits, pictures of the whole family gathered together, side by side, united. We look at family portraits and remember how much each family member means to us. When one of these family members passes away, the portrait stands as a reminder of their life, value, and connectedness to the whole family.

In this portion of Colossians, the apostle Paul is painting a family portrait, a picture of his spiritual family. Each person matters, each one is connected as a brother or sister, each one is loved. As you read these verses, allow the portrait of these faithful followers of Christ to be painted in your heart and mind. Remember, these people were not just Paul's family, but your family as well.

What is it about this person's life that strikes you?

9. Describe one person in your family portrait of faith and why he or she means so much to you.

10. If someone was to describe you as being in their family portrait of faith, what would you hope they would say?

Celebrating and Being Celebrated

We can all look back and identify specific people who have prayed for us and helped us grow as followers of Christ. Take time to pray together and celebrate the influence these people have had in your life. Remember it is no accident that these people have been part of your journey of faith; God placed them there to help you along the way. Thank Him for these people and how they have made your faith deeper and richer.

Loving and Being Loved

The apostle Paul gives us a wonderful portrait of his brothers and sisters in Christ. When you read Colossians 4:7–17, you can see Paul's deep love for these people and his desire to build them up and affirm them.

Too often we can be careless with our words and tear others down rather than build them up. As we saw at the beginning of this study, our words have the power of life and death. James warns us that, like a fire, our words can burn. With all of this in mind, humbly reflect back over the past weeks. If you have spoken harshly to someone, commit yourself to go back to them and seek restoration. Where you were out of line, ask for forgiveness. Where they were in the wrong, extend forgiveness. Invite a member of your small group to pray for you as you seek healing in this relationship, and have them keep you accountable to follow through on this commitment.

Serving and Being Served

Paul asks the Colossian Christians to pray faithfully for his evangelistic work and ask for God to open doors. He asks them to pray for him to speak with absolute clarity. And Paul hungers for a boldness that will only come when God's people pray.

Commit as a group to adopt one missionary as an honorary member of your small group. Lift up these three prayers every time you gather:

1. Heavenly Father, go before this person and open doors for Your Word to touch hearts and change lives.
2. Jesus Christ, anoint this person's lips to speak with great clarity and conviction.
3. Spirit of God, fill them with boldness and courage, to stand strong no matter what they face.

You might want to agree on a missionary who is a personal friend of a group member, or someone your congregation supports. Seek to stay in touch with this person, and if they are ever traveling near your church, invite them to spend an evening with your small group.

Session One — A New Look at the Church
COLOSSIANS 1:1–14

Question 1

In a day and age when many people are walking away from dying or stagnant churches, there are many reasons people are drawn to churches that are biblically functioning communities. As a matter of fact, when the church is all God wants it to be, people find themselves drawn to it in ways they often can't explain. God made us to be in community, and when a church breathes the life of real community, people want to be a part of it. Take time as a group to describe what keeps you connected and a part of your local church.

Question 2

It has been said, "If you find the perfect church, don't join it. Because, when you join, it will no longer be perfect." This is not meant to be insulting, but simply a reminder that there are no perfect people, and therefore, no perfect churches. However, we can dream and envision what an ideal church might look like. Dream together as a group and discuss what a church might look like if it was truly functioning as the Bible says a community of Christians should function. What would be essential, and what would not be part of this church? Remember, the goal is not to envision our idea of a perfect church, but to get inside of God's vision for a biblically functioning community of believers.

Questions 3–6

Trademark #1 — Simple Faith (v. 4).

The truth is, the church is not a building. It is not a social structure for baptisms, marriages, and funerals. The church is not a performance by the clergy. It is not a positive-thinking rally. It is not a group therapy session. It is not a theological synod. It is not a soul-winning station. It is not a Bible study. Instead, the church is a collection of people who have a simple faith and trust in Jesus Christ. Although churches might do many of these things listed above and reflect some of these activities, the church is not any of them. It is the gathered people of God!

Paul said that the number one trademark of a biblically functioning community is a real and simple faith in Christ. When this faith exists, there is joy and health. When this trademark has disappeared, the group of people gathered are no longer the church. If faith in Christ is not the foundation, the whole structure is unsound.

Trademark #2 — Love for One Another (v. 4).

The true test of whether or not there is a real church and real faith is whether or not there is real love.

When I was growing up, love was not a core concern when it came to knowing what the church was all about. In the church of my childhood, here was the question: How do you know if it is a real church? Here was the answer: If the people knew the answers to specific belief-oriented questions, if they agreed with our doctrines, and if they could quote the right Bible verses. This was the test of a true church.

I never bought it. I have discovered that people can know the answers, quote the verses, and regurgitate the doctrines with absolute clarity, and still not have the love of Christ alive in their heart or church. If the love of Christ does not, at some time, melt your heart, so that you become a lover of people, there is something dramatically wrong with the church. I have gone so far as to say that the true test of orthodoxy is the transformation of attitudes and relationships. Remember the words from the first letter of John:

> *If anyone says, "I love God," yet hates his brother, he is a liar. For anyone who does not love his brother, whom he has seen, cannot love God, whom he has not seen. And he has given us this command: Whoever loves God must also love his brother.*
>
> (1 John 4:20–21)

This is not to say that doctrine and biblical truth are not core and critical for our faith. However, adherence to a set of beliefs is not the whole story. When we truly know God's Word and the powerful truth it communicates, and when we enter a genuine relationship with the Jesus Christ revealed in the Bible and become His followers, our beliefs will transform our lifestyles, and we will become lovers of people. This is the model of our Savior.

The second mark of a true church is a sensitive, compassionate love for one another. Love has a way of proving that we really know Christ. I have learned over the years that people rarely stay in a church because of the pastors, music, or facilities. They stay because they are loved. The world cannot refute love!

This love is not just some gooey feeling of sentimentality. True love is about helping each other through self-sacrifice. It's about us making your problem my problem. Service and sacrifice are at the core of the love we show for each other.

Trademark #3 — A Hope in Heaven (v. 5).

Christians, more than anyone, should *not* be tied to the things of this world. If we believe Christ has been raised and if we live with the hope of heaven, then we will keep our eyes on eternal matters. What are eternal treasures? People! What really matters in this life? People. We need to care for them, love them, and point them toward Christ. A church that is functioning according to biblical guidelines will not get tangled up in all the stuff of this world, but will keep its focus on what is eternal.

Trademark #4 — Fruit-Bearing (v. 6).

One essential trademark of a biblically functioning community is lives that bear fruit. There will be activity, transformation, and lives that are radically committed to Christ. In the Sermon on the Mount, Jesus said you will know His followers by their fruit!

How does a life change? How does fruit grow? When a heart is transformed by the Word of God or an agent of God, which is us! It happens when we look into the mirror, speak the truth about ourselves, and ask God to recreate us and make us into who He wants us to be. This fruit-bearing is not just private, but it is corporate and very, very public. Others need to see the fruit that grows in the life of a follower of Christ.

Trademark #5 — Faithful Signposts (Like Epaphras) (v. 7-8).

In any great movement, church, or ministry, you will find great individuals. These are people who can envision what God can do through the life of a person. We all need to ask the questions, "What do I mean to the church? Where do I fit? How has God gifted and wired me for ministry?" When we answer these questions and begin to offer our lives in service, we can become like Epaphras, a faithful signpost for others to see.

The church needs to be filled with individuals who allow God to do miracles through them. That's why every person counts. No matter what gifts you have or how you use them to serve others, you are more important than you might ever dream. You might set up equipment, teach Sunday school, lead a small group, serve on the board, help in the nursery, or do any of a hundred other ministries, but you need to realize that this is your place and an expression of your function as a member of the body of Christ.

Questions 7–10

In this brief prayer for the followers of Christ in Colosse, Paul lifts up four specific prayers.

Paul prays for them to be filled with the knowledge of God's will (v. 9).

The Colossians had a great start. The church was growing, honoring Christ, and reaching out to others. Everything looked great. Paul and Timothy knew that this was not the time to stop praying, but to intensify their prayer activity on behalf of this young congregation. With this in mind, they prayed for the Colossian Christians to grow deeper and deeper in their knowledge of Jesus and His will for their lives.

I can say categorically that when followers of Christ put a premium on ignorance, they don't know what they are doing. They are cutting themselves off from the most intimate, deepest relationships they could ever develop with the God of the universe. In order for your love for God to grow, your knowledge of Him must grow. Knowledge does not grow on trees, or come easily. We hunger for it. We seek it. We grow in it. (For the relationship between wisdom and knowledge, see Proverbs 1–4.)

This is why followers of Christ gather weekly to study the Word of God and seek His knowledge. This is why we read God's word on a daily basis. Any mature follower of Christ knows this and hungers to know God's will more and more.

Too often people say, "I can't seem to love God in a real deep way." Yet when you know Him more and more, your love for Him will grow. As we grow to know Him and love Him, we long to obey Him. It comes naturally. When we know of the death of Christ for us, the demands of Christ begin to make sense. Here is a simple, yet profound reality: The more we know Him (not just know about Him), the more we will love Him.

Paul prays for them to live a life worthy of the Lord (v. 10).

Later in the book of Colossians Paul writes:

Therefore, as God's chosen people, holy and dearly loved, clothe yourselves with compassion, kindness, humility, gentleness and patience. Bear with each other and forgive whatever grievances you may have against one another. Forgive as the Lord forgave you. And over all these virtues put on love, which binds them all together in perfect unity.

(Colossians 3:12–14)

We all need to grow in how we live our lives of love and our moral lives. These are inseparable. We can have a lot of love, but we need a lot of purity also. Paul prays for the Colossian Christians to have lives that reflect the very heart and will of God. This should be our prayer for ourselves and for other followers of Christ. God's standard is high, but we should never stop striving upward in how we live our lives.

Paul prays for them to be strengthened with God's power (v. 11).

Strength, power, might, endurance, and *patience*—all of these words appear in this one verse. Paul longs for the Christians in this new church in Colosse to have God's power to hang in there. Paul knows the weariness that can come with standing up for Christ in a hostile world. Remember, Paul had been beaten, mistreated, and imprisoned for his faith. He knew it was no cakewalk. Prayer for strength and endurance for followers of Christ is as needed today as it was two thousand years ago.

Paul prays for them to live with a profound understanding of their inheritance (v. 12).

We need to learn to give thanks for the inheritance we have in Christ. God is not asking for a painted-on smile and a practiced "Praise the Lord" for every crisis in life. However, true followers of Christ live with a moment-by-moment conviction that heaven is their home and what lies ahead is far greater than anything we experience in this life. Our inheritance is secure, so we can freely leverage our time, abilities, and resources in Christ's work here on earth.

Session Two — A New Look at Jesus
COLOSSIANS 1:15–27

Question 1

Many of us can remember times when we were passionately in love with Jesus. There was an innocence and excitement that brought joy and meaning to life. But with time we have gotten away from this first love. We are busy serving Jesus, but we don't have time to be with Jesus. This is not God's plan for our lives.

He wants us to keep Him as our first love at all times. He wants us to know that this is not just something we should hope for, but something we can experience. Sometimes looking back to those times of great intimacy and closeness helps trigger a desire and commitment to get back to our first love. Take time as a group to reflect back on some of those high points in your lives as Christ followers.

Questions 2–3

Many people say things like, "I wonder what God is like" or "I don't think God would ever do that" or "I think that if God were here He would say this." I hear so much conjecture about who God is and what He is like. People waste time trying to use their own abilities to figure out the character of God. In this passage Paul tells us that Jesus Christ is the exact representation of God. If we want to know the heart of God, we need to look at the heart of Jesus. If we wonder what God would do, we need to look at the action of Jesus. Jesus Christ is the perfect reflection of the heart and character of our heavenly Father.

He is also the firstborn of all creation. This does not mean that Jesus has a beginning, but instead points to the pre-existence of Christ. Jesus is the agent of creation, the One through whom all things were made (John 1:3). He created everything, and He is the One who can love, redeem, forgive, and recreate this broken world.

When we give, serve, sing, or minister in any way, it's not for us, but for Jesus. When we love, we do it in the name of Christ. He is the head of the church, and we are His body. We need to keep this perspective so that we never overestimate ourselves and underestimate Jesus.

He is the firstborn from the dead. When He rose, He paved the way for all who believe in Him to be resurrected. He broke the chains of death. He crushed the power of sin. He opened the door to eternity with God. All who believe in Him live with the hope of resurrection.

Jesus has first place in everything. He is the CEO of the whole universe! Paul puts it this way:

> Therefore God exalted him to the highest place
> and gave him the name that is above every name,
> that at the name of Jesus every knee should bow,
> in heaven and on earth and under the earth,
> and every tongue confess that Jesus Christ is Lord,
> to the glory of God the Father.

(Philippians 2:9–11)

Jesus is first in the universe, nations, governments, and the church. He is also first in our families. Christ should be the guest at every table. He rules over the relationships between spouses and parents and children. We need to yield the control of our homes and families over to Him.

Most important of all, Jesus must be first in our lives. We all need to ask the question, Who is on the throne of my life? Who is first? It must be Christ! Not money, power, relationships, accomplishments, entertainment, food, personal achievement, or anything else. Our answer to this question influences every aspect of our lives. Christ must be in charge of everything.

Jesus wanted people to know who He was. He said things like:

> "Don't you know me, Philip, even after I have been among you such a long time? Anyone who has seen me has seen the Father. How can you say, 'Show us the Father'?"

(John 14:9)

> "I and the Father are one."

(John 10:30)

> "You are from below; I am from above. You are of this world; I am not of this world. I told you that you would die in your sins; if you do not believe that I am the one I claim to be, you will indeed die in your sins."

(John 8:23–24)

Question 4

Jesus Christ is the One who holds all things together. He is the glue the universe depends on for cohesiveness. He is a cosmic adhesive. What keeps the seasons changing? What keeps the planets from bumping into each other? What makes the whole universe move in perfect unison, like a flawless ballet? Jesus. He holds it all together. If Jesus removed His sustaining hand from creation, it would collapse back into a shapeless void.

Question 5

Jesus is the head of the church. There was no question that Epaphras was a great leader. But Jesus, and only Jesus, is the head of the church. Pastors, boards, big money members, movers and shakers—they all bow their knees together before Jesus. We don't follow a personality, but a crucified and risen Savior. When anyone else tries to take this place of supremacy, we break the heart of our Savior and work against His will for our lives and His church.

Questions 7–11

Jesus wants to take people who are alienated and hostile and love them back to the Father. He wants to present them blameless and beyond reproach. He wants to turn strangers into children of God, slaves into free people, debtors into heirs, and enemies into friends. He wants to take lives soiled and ruined by sin and make them spotless and clean.

This is as dramatic a reversal as our minds can comprehend. Outside of Christ we are alienated, enemies of God and evil in our behaviors. Not a pretty picture. But when we are honest with ourselves and God, we have to admit that it is a fair portrayal of our lives without Christ.

But when we become followers of Christ, everything changes. We become holy, spotless, free from any accusation. God looks on us and sees no sin, defect, or charge against us.

What has happened?

We have been reconciled to God through Christ's physical body (His death on the cross) and cleansed by His blood (Colossians 1:20, 22). Only through Christ can this happen.

This is our one hope for cleansing and a whole new beginning. This is how we can change from who we are to who we were meant to be.

Paul uses strong and pointed language. He draws dramatic contrasts between what we were and what we become in Christ. Why? Because there is no greater contrast in all of creation. A person without Christ, and the same person with Christ, are like two entirely different people. This is why Jesus calls this transformation being "born again" (John 3:3). A whole new life has begun.

Session Three — A New Foundation
COLOSSIANS 1:28–2:23

Question 1

In our day and age it seems like people are trying to build their lives on almost anything except Jesus Christ. Money, personal accomplishments, fame, relationships, and worldly philosophies are just a few of the sand-like foundations on which people build. What we need to learn is that any and all foundations, except Christ, will eventually crumble.

Question 2

Paul had a passionate love for the church. This was not a love for a building, a specific denomination, or even a particular theological bias. It was a gut-level, affectionate, emotional response to a precious group of human beings who had humbly received Christ. Paul saw a group of brand new followers of Christ who had traded in their brokenness for His healing. Paul saw that these new believers were trading in everything for Christ, and he wanted them to know that he would do anything to help them grow in faith.

Look closely at Paul's language. He is passionately proclaiming, admonishing, teaching, and struggling on their behalf. The word *struggling*, at its core, has the sense of agonizing. Paul is ready to pour his self out for these new Christ followers. They are babies in their faith, and he is ready to stand by them as they grow to maturity. We need to share in this kind of commitment to help new believers grow into fully devoted followers of Christ.

Questions 3–4

Jesus Christ is the only foundation worth building on. He is the One who can encourage us, unite us, and give us understanding of what really matters in life. Faith in Him is firm, solid, and lasting.

Jesus Christ causes our roots to grow deep and secure, like a tree planted by a rich water source (Psalm 1). When we are rooted in Christ, we draw our very life from Him. If we are cut off from the living water of His presence, our lives begin to wither and die.

At the same time, we are built up in Jesus Christ. Like a master carpenter, Jesus works on our lives making us exactly what He wants us to be. This image gives a window into how much our lives rely on Jesus Christ. First, He is the foundation on which our lives are built. Then, He moves in our lives by the Holy Spirit and builds us up in faith.

Paul also writes of how we are strengthened in our faith. In our fast-paced world, some people have a personal trainer who comes to their home or workplace and walks them through a regular workout program. Jesus wants to function in this capacity in our lives. We need regular exercise of our spiritual muscles to stay strong and healthy. Jesus is ready to offer a workout that will strengthen us and keep us in shape for the life He wants us to live.

Questions 6–8

Paul offers a warning that is loud and clear. We live in a world with a smorgasbord of deceptive philosophies. He wants us to be keenly aware that we are all susceptible to the enticements of the world. They clamor to gain our attention, move into our hearts, and take captive our lives. This verse is a signpost in the road of life telling us to beware! We need to guard our minds. We need to scrutinize the philosophies of this world and be sure we are not buying into a lie.

We live in a day when tolerance is lifted up as the ultimate good. We are told that we can't know absolute truth, and we certainly should never impose "our truth" on others. Every life philosophy is given affirmation, and people are encouraged to create their own truth system. If it works for them, it is acceptable.

Yet, as followers of Christ, we need to learn how to discern what is false and stand against it. Materialism is held up as a good worldview and greed is seen as healthy. Yet Jesus calls us to surrender all we have to Him! New Age philosophies and revamped Eastern mysticism is growing in popularity. Science is held up as the final authority, and intellectualism is seen as the enlightened way to see the world. Yet in all of this, Christ alone offers a lasting foundation. All other world religions fall short. All other philosophies ring hollow. All other foundations will erode with time. We need to honestly call these deceptive philosophies what they are: a delusion, a mirage, a faulty foundation.

Paul calls out to the Colossians and through history to us: Jesus can set you free from all false philosophies and teachings. He is God in human flesh. He has power over every authority in all of creation. Through His death and resurrection, every enemy has been defeated, every false philosophy disarmed, every power broken. We can be set free in Him alone.

Questions 9–10

In the first century, there were certain external religious practices that gave many people a false sense of security and religious pride: dietary laws (v. 16), observation of specific festivals and celebrations (v. 16), Sabbath practices (v. 16), worship of angels (v. 18), visions (v. 18), and asceticism (harsh treatment of the body) (v. 23). For many people, a life devoted to Christ was not their focus, but observance of all the rules and regulations. Rather than living authentic lives as followers of Christ, they were following man-made rules that caused bondage rather than freedom.

In our day the same problem exists. The behaviors might look a little different, but the problem is still the same. There are people who have traded in life as a devoted follower of Christ for a life devoted to rules and religious regulations. They know all the answers on the Bible quiz, but they don't know Jesus. Often the surface behaviors are good, but they are not growing out of a sincere relationship. People attend church (sometimes more than once a week), they put money in the offering plate, they might even be part of a small group, but these things can simply be legalistic behaviors performed to gain God's favor.

It seems various church traditions have their own set of do's and don'ts that define if a person is truly one of the faithful. Do you drink? Do you smoke? Do you attend church twice on Sunday? Do you play cards? Do you gamble? Do you shop on Sunday? Do you read your Bible for at least fifteen minutes each morning? Do you dance? Do you, do you, do you . . .

As soon as we base our faith on a list of do's and don'ts, rather than on Jesus, we are in trouble. Once we become devoted followers of Christ, we may very well have to face some of these questions, and we very well might end up changing the way we live in a willing response to God's love for us. But no legal system, no matter how religious it might seem, will ever lead to a person experiencing new life. Only a relationship with Jesus can do this.

Session Four — A Whole New You
COLOSSIANS 3:1–17

Question 1

We all have people in our lives whom we love and respect deeply. Their opinion and affirmation can mean a great deal. Take time to discuss these people and why their view of you matters so much. Remember, it is not wrong to respect or care about the opinions of others. However, we should never be ruled by their perspective on who we are. And in the midst of all of this, we need to learn that God's perspective on who we are matters most of all.

Question 2

Paul is clear that we are made complete in Christ. We are not saved by Christ plus works, or Christ plus good intentions, or Christ plus knowledge, or Christ plus anything. We have forgiveness of our sins through Christ alone. In these chapters, Paul passionately teaches us about positional theology. In

Christ, we have everything we need. Our position is secure. No one and nothing can change this reality.

If we learn to see ourselves the way God sees us, we will be overwhelmed! In Christ we are holy, reconciled, forgiven, freed from any accusation, and loved beyond description. Try to get your mind around this reality. Learn to care more about what God thinks about you than what anyone else says or thinks.

Questions 3–4

Positional theology always gives way to principles of practical Christian living. In other words, our new position in Christ changes us. Once we know what we have in Christ, we are to live accordingly. Our way of thinking and the motives of our heart change dramatically. Nothing is the same, because our hearts are changed. Even when we do the same outward actions, our inner person is acting this way with new and pure motives. We stop doing things so that we look good, and we long for God's glory and are concerned for others.

As we look in the mirror, we need to be honest with ourselves. We have a new position in Christ, and we are called to a new mind-set and heart condition, but sometimes, we remain unchanged. We can speak of being focused on the things of God, but often our focus is almost exclusively on the things of this world. But when our hearts and minds are truly changed and infused with the presence of God's Spirit, our actions begin to change. This is what Paul addresses in the coming verses.

Question 5

After teaching us about our new position in Christ and calling us to a new attitude (heart and mind condition), Paul now begins to address the critical topic of changed actions. Because we are loved, forgiven, reconciled, and holy, our lives should look different. There are some behaviors that need to stop, some actions that do not honor Christ and have no place in the life of His follower.

Paul exhorts the believer to strip off the actions of the old self. It is important to remember the the eleven sins he mentions are only examples. These sins illustrate the need for change, but there are hundreds more examples that could be given. These are not some secret eleven sins to avoid but represent the need for ongoing surrender of every area of our lives to God.

Question 6

Paul could have addressed any sin first, but he started with temptation to sexual sin, "sexual immorality, impurity and lust." Sometimes we falsely think that abuse of human sexuality is some new invention crafted by purveyors of pornography and Internet virtual sex. Not so. Sexual sin goes back before Sodom and Gomorrah. Sinful men and women will always be tempted by this powerful force, and followers of Christ are called to submit their desire to God's plan for human sexuality. One reason Paul might have addressed this first is that there is no person who walks this earth that does not have to grapple with what it means to honor Christ with their sexuality.

In a sex-crazed and insanely permissive culture, there are countless windows, doors, and secret entryways for sin to invade our hearts, minds, and lives. We need to be honest about this and learn to close off these sources of temptation as much as possible. We must regulate the magazines we buy, the movies we see, the books we read, and the TV shows that shape our thinking. In a video, cable, and Internet-friendly world, there are new enemies to face. Pornographic images that were unimaginable just decades ago are now as close as the click of a mouse or the touch of a remote control. All of these can now be wired into our homes with absolute anonymity. But their influence will be etched on our souls for years to come.

As followers of Christ we need to learn how to cut off the source of temptation. If that means ordering a filter on your Internet service, getting rid of a few channels on your cable service, or avoiding certain places, so be it! God calls us to strip off this old way of living and to honor Him with our minds and bodies.

Question 7

We all know the children's taunt, "Sticks and stones can break my bones, but words will never hurt me." But we also know how wrong this taunt is. Sticks and stones can break our bones, but words can kill us! We have all felt the knife thrust of hurtful words. When others slander us, lie about us, or curse us, we feel it deeply. When we use our words to damage others, we betray that we still have much to learn about living as followers of Christ.

Questions 8–10

Again, Paul does not attempt to list every item in the new wardrobe of a Christ follower. But he does take a few items off the shelves and racks as examples of the change that happens in people when they become believers. The old clothing is stripped away, and new clothing is given.

In the first century, there was a literal parallel. When people became Christ followers, they would go down into the waters of baptism in their old garments. When they came up out of the water, they received clean white robes, a sign of their new life in Christ.

Paul is now reminding the Colossian Christians, and us, that we are to take on a whole new life in Christ. We now wear compassion, kindness, humility, gentleness, patience, forgiveness, love, unity, peace, thankfulness, worship, and every other good thing we have in Christ. It is a process, but as we grow into fully devoted followers of Christ, we wear these things more and more. And the things of our old life continue to be stripped off.

Session Five — A New Look at Relationships
COLOSSIANS 3:18–4:1

Question 1

As we enter this session, it is important to note that Paul is being direct and bold in his teaching. He is not giving light-hearted advice that the Colossian Christians can take or leave at their own whim. He is hammering home some essential truth for healthy, Christ-honoring relationships in the home.

Too many of us live a double life. We present ourselves one way when we are among God's people, but in the private retreat of our home, we are someone else entirely. This Jekyll and Hyde existence needs to come to an end. Our family members should not have lots of little secrets and surprises they could tell about us. Our lives should be so consistent that the way we appear when we gather for worship with God's people is consistent with how we conduct ourselves in our homes.

Question 2

Our coworkers see us for forty to fifty hours a week. They see us manage stress, deal with tough situations, and respond on the fly. Do your best to see yourself through the eyes of your coworkers. How do they see you? What would they say about you? If you suspect that it would not be greatly flattering, consider changing your actions to reflect the heart of Jesus.

If you feel particularly bold, you might even want to ask coworkers to give an honest evaluation of how they see you in the workplace. Use their insight to help affirm where you are doing well, and to give direction for areas where you need to grow.

Questions 3–5

This is not intended to be a thorough doctoral dissertation from the apostle Paul plumbing the ocean depths for every hidden truth concerning what it takes to build a family. It is only meant to be a brief and very direct shot at the core of what it takes to live out the Christian faith within a family. These are very practical principles that are presented clearly here, and in many other places in the Old and New Testament. It might be helpful to look at Ephesians 5:21–6:9 as you reflect on this passage.

These exhortations are framed with a parallel. This appears here, and also in Ephesians 5:21–6:9. Paul uses the term, "as is fitting in the Lord" (Colossians 3:18). We need to remember that God cares deeply about how we treat each other. Our family relationships can bring honor to God.

Wives (v. 18)

Some women react negatively to these words. There are even scholars who try to say that Paul is calling wives to submit to their husbands only when their husband's desires are consistent with their own. In other words, submit when you agree with him. Some also try to make this a cultural issue that no longer applies today. I have to disagree.

At the same time, wives should not read into this passage what is not there. Paul does not say that wives have to obey their husbands in every situation, no matter what, as they grovel at their husband's feet. This is not the sense of what Paul is trying to communicate. This is not the intention of the word *submit*.

Rather, the sense of this word is a quiet, cooperative desire of a wife to please her husband. There is a sense of a loving partnership—not a forced or coerced response. Wives should so love and respect their husbands that they want to work in harmonious cooperation.

It is important to realize that this submission is not an issue of inferiority. In the New Testament we read that Christ submitted to the Father. Yet we know that Jesus is still equal to the Father. In the same way, a wife does not lose her dignity or integrity when she submits to her husband. Rather, it is a powerful and outward expression of love and honor, and an example of the mutual submission to which we are all called (see Ephesians 5:21).

Husbands (v. 19)

Again Ephesians gives us additional insight on this topic. In Ephesians 5:25 husbands are called to love their wives the way Jesus loved the church and died for her. This is our model. This is our example. This is the standard to which we aspire.

Humble and sacrificial service should mark the life of every husband who is a follower of Christ. Remember that the church consumed Jesus' life, and it meant His death. Jesus gave everything for the church, His bride.

Sadly, too many husbands give their wives the leftovers. Many husbands, even those who are in relationship with Jesus

Christ, toss their wives leftover time, leftover money, and leftover affection. When husbands get consumed with their own goals, careers, hobbies, and desires, wives get neglected. In the face of this reality, Paul calls husbands to readjust their schedules and priorities to put their wives on the top of the list, just like the church was on the top of Jesus' list.

This is a love that must be expressed in gentleness. There is no room for harshness in the way a husband relates to his wife. Rather, tender words, touch, and even looks are essential.

Children and Parents (vv. 20–21)

God is not only concerned about the relationships of husbands and wives, but also the relationship between children and parents. Paul addresses the fifth of the Ten Commandments:

> *Honor your father and your mother, so that you may live long in the land the LORD your God is giving you.*
> (Exodus 20:12)

Paul reminds children that God expects them to respect and obey their parents. This is not about a mindless adherence to every demand and whim of a cruel parent. Rather, it is about a humble respect for parents, a respect that shapes the response patterns of children. Parents who seek to love and lead their children should be met with a willing spirit, not resistance at every turn.

In the same way, parents should do all they can to keep relationships good with their children. Parents need to avoid doing those things which push their kids' buttons and frustrate them. Parents should not try to force every child into the same mold. This only frustrates and embitters them. A wise parent will know each child well enough to care for him or her in a way that fits their unique temperament.

Questions 6–7

These questions will not apply to everyone. Not every member of every small group will be married or have children. However, we can all reflect on ways we can grow as followers of Christ that will help us have Christ-honoring relationships in our home.

Questions 8–10

It is critically important to realize that Paul is not teaching directly about employees, employers, or the workplace. However, there are parallels that can be drawn. Employees should heed the call to labor with excellence, integrity, and as to the Lord. Also, those in leadership and management in the workplace need to treat others with respect and dignity. Our God cares deeply about righteousness and justice in human relationships.

Those who are followers of Christ, and who also happen to be employers, need to remember this as they work with others. They will answer to God for how they have treated those who work for them. The same umbrella principle applies to those who are employees and those who are employers—do all you do as if you were doing it for the Lord.

Session Six—A New Voice
COLOSSIANS 4:2–18

Questions 2–4

The Bible says, whatever you do as a follower of Christ, learn to pray. This is the language that best reflects our position in Christ. Once we are in the family, we need to learn to talk with the Father often and regularly. Here is a small sampling of calls to prayer in the New Testament:

> *Be always on the watch, and pray that you may be able to escape all that is about to happen, and that you may be able to stand before the Son of Man.*
>
> (Luke 21:36)

> *Be joyful in hope, patient in affliction, faithful in prayer.*
>
> (Romans 12:12)

> *Do not be anxious about anything, but in everything, by prayer and petition, with thanksgiving, present your requests to God. And the peace of God, which transcends all understanding, will guard your hearts and your minds*

in Christ Jesus.

(Philippians 4:6–7)

And pray in the Spirit on all occasions with all kinds of prayers and requests. With this in mind, be alert and always keep on praying for all the saints.

(Ephesians 6:18)

Be joyful always; pray continually; give thanks in all circumstances, for this is God's will for you in Christ Jesus.

(1 Thessalonians 5:16–18)

Prayer might seem like an unnatural activity to a new believer, but to a fully devoted follower of Christ, it becomes a natural part of every day, and every moment.

Paul speaks of watchful prayer, thankful prayer, and prayers of supplication (praying for the needs of others). Yet the Bible is filled with all kinds of other prayer expressions: confession (Psalm 51), laments (Psalm 22), praise for who God is (Psalm 92)—the list goes on and on. We need to learn that there is great breadth to the landscape of prayer.

Paul calls us to regular and focused prayer for the issues of the church as well as for our lives as followers of Christ. He also invites us to lift up spontaneous prayer throughout our day.

Questions 5–7

Paul does not cover the whole topic of evangelism in this passage. But he does give some very helpful instructions for Christ followers as we are in relationship with those who don't have faith in Jesus.

He calls us to wisdom in our actions with seekers. The truth is, they are watching us. Our attitudes, words, and actions are on display for the whole world to see. We might feel this is unfair and puts undue pressure on us, but the reality is that our actions have great impact on seekers. We need to reflect the heart, love, and grace of Christ in all of our actions. We need to slow down and get a little introspective. We need to ask, how will my non-believing friend take this? What message will I send?

We also need to look for opportunities to tell others about God's love and the news that Jesus Christ loves them. This is not a forceful attack on their privacy. We simply need to realize that God opens doors of opportunity, and we need to walk through them. We need to tune in to how the Holy Spirit is working, and learn to follow. If you want to discover your own personal style for communicating naturally about your faith, you might want to investigate the book and curriculum *Becoming a Contagious Christian*, published by Zondervan Publishing House.

Many Christ followers want to know how to explain their faith and defend it with clarity, but they are not sure where to start. If your small group has a real interest in this topic, consider looking into the Tough Questions small group curriculum from Willow Creek Resources, published by Zondervan. This might be a good follow-up to this study of Colossians.

Questions 8–9

Paul paints a beautiful portrait of a family of faith. Take time as a group to get to know these followers of Christ who lived in the first century. They are part of an eternal family that includes every follower of Christ throughout all of history.

As you read, get a sense for Paul's love, admiration, and affirmation of these brothers and sisters. Let this portrait encourage you to be a person who is quick to affirm and bless others who love God and follow Jesus. Use this time to affirm and uplift some of your small group members.

Willow Creek Association

Vision, Training, Resources for Prevailing Churches

This resource was created to serve you and to help you build a local church that prevails. It is just one of many ministry tools that are part of the Willow Creek Resources® line, published by the Willow Creek Association together with Zondervan.

The Willow Creek Association (WCA) was created in 1992 to serve a rapidly growing number of churches from across the denominational spectrum that are committed to helping unchurched people become fully devoted followers of Christ. Membership in the WCA now numbers over 10,000 Member Churches worldwide from more than ninety denominations.

The Willow Creek Association links like-minded Christian leaders with each other and with strategic vision, training, and resources in order to help them build prevailing churches designed to reach their redemptive potential. Here are some of the ways the WCA does that.

- **Prevailing Church Conference**—an annual two-and-a-half day event, held at Willow Creek Community Church in South Barrington, Illinois, to help pioneering church leaders raise up a volunteer core while discovering new and innovative ways to build prevailing churches that reach unchurched people.

- **Leadership Summit**—a once-a-year, two-and-a-half-day conference to envision and equip Christians with leadership gifts and responsibilities. Presented live at Willow Creek as well as via satellite broadcast to over sixty locations across North America, this event is designed to increase the leadership effectiveness of pastors, ministry staff, volunteer church leaders, and Christians in the marketplace.

- **Ministry-Specific Conferences**—throughout each year the WCA hosts a variety of conferences and training events—both at Willow Creek's main campus and offsite, across the U.S. and around the world—targeting church leaders in ministry-specific areas such as: evangelism, the arts, children, students, small groups, preaching and teaching, spiritual formation, spiritual gifts, raising up resources, etc.

- **Willow Creek Resources**®—to provide churches with trusted and field-tested ministry resources in such areas as leadership, evangelism, spiritual formation, spiritual gifts, small groups, stewardship, student ministry, children's ministry, the use of the arts—drama, media, contemporary music—and more. For additional information about Willow Creek Resources® call the Customer Service Center at 800-570-9812. Outside the U.S. call 847-765-0070.

- *WillowNet*—the WCA's Internet resource service, which provides access to hundreds of transcripts of Willow Creek messages, drama scripts, songs, videos, and multimedia tools. The system allows users to sort through these elements and download them for a fee. Visit us online at www.willowcreek.com.

- **WCA News**—a quarterly publication to inform you of the latest trends, resources, and information on WCA events from around the world.

- *Defining Moments*—a monthly audio journal for church leaders featuring Bill Hybels and other Christian leaders discussing probing issues to help you discover biblical principles and transferable strategies to maximize your church's redemptive potential.

- *The Exchange*—our online classified ads service to assist churches in recruiting key staff for ministry positions.

- **Member Benefits**—includes substantial discounts to WCA training events, a 20 percent discount on all Willow Creek Resources®, access to a Members-Only section on WillowNet, monthly communications, and more. Member Churches also receive special discounts and premier services through WCA's growing number of ministry partners—Select Service Providers.

For specific information about WCA membership, upcoming conferences, and other ministry services contact:

Willow Creek Association
P.O. Box 3188, Barrington, IL 60011-3188
Phone: 847-570-9812
Fax: 847-765-5046
www.willowcreek.com

Walk with God Together
Walking With God Series
Don Cousins and Judson Poling

This series of six guides (and two leader's guides) provides a solid, biblical program of study for all of the small groups in your church. The Walking With God Series is designed to help lead new and young believers into a deeper personal intimacy with God, while at the same time building a strong foundation in the faith for all believers, regardless of their level of maturity. These guides are also appropriate for individual study. Titles in the series are:

Friendship with God: Developing Intimacy with God	0-310-59143-0
The Incomparable Jesus: Experiencing the Power of Christ	0-310-59153-8
"Follow Me!": Walking with Jesus in Everyday Life	0-310-59163-5
Leader's Guide 1 (covers these first three books)	0-310-59203-8
Discovering Your Church: Becoming Part of God's New Community	0-310-59173-2
Building Your Church: Using Your Gifts, Time, and Resources	0-310-59183-X
Impacting Your World: Becoming a Person of Influence	0-310-59193-7
Leader's Guide 2 (covers these last three books)	0-310-59213-5
Also available: *Walking With God Journal*	0-310-91642-9

Look for the Walking With God Series
at your local Christian bookstore.

WILLOW
Willow Creek Resources

www.willowcreek.com

ZONDERVAN™

GRAND RAPIDS, MICHIGAN 49530 USA
WWW.ZONDERVAN.COM

Not sure about joining a new community?
The Case for Christ
Lee Strobel

Is there credible evidence that Jesus of Nazareth really is the Son of God?

Retracing his own spiritual journey from atheism to faith, Lee Strobel, former legal editor of the *Chicago Tribune*, cross-examines a dozen experts with doctorates from schools like Cambridge, Princeton, and Brandeis who are recognized authorities in their own fields.

Strobel challenges them with questions like *How reliable is the New Testament? Does evidence exist for Jesus outside the Bible? Is there any reason to believe the resurrection was an actual event?*

Strobel's tough, point-blank questions make this remarkable book read like a captivating, fast-paced novel. But it's not fiction. It's a riveting quest for the truth about history's most compelling figure.

What will your verdict be in *The Case for Christ?*

Hardcover: 0-310-22646-5
Softcover: 0-310-20930-7
Audio Pages: 0-310-21960-4

Available at your local Christian bookstore.

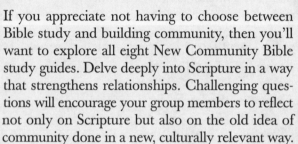

Bring your group to a deeper level of interaction!
InterActions Series
Bill Hybels

Help your small-group members help each other develop into fully devoted followers of Christ. InterActions discussion guides ask for a deeper level of sharing, creating lines of accountability between individuals and moving your group into action. Each book presents six thought-provoking sessions specifically designed to build on the dynamics and interplay of small groups.

Essential Christianity: Practical Steps for Spiritual Growth	0-310-21317-7
Getting a Grip: Finding Balance in Your Daily Life	0-310-21318-5
Overcoming: Applying God's Power Where You Need It Most	0-310-21717-2
Serving Lessons: Putting God and Others First	0-310-21315-0
Authenticity: Being Honest with God and Others	0-310-20674-X
Commitment: Developing Deeper Devotion to Christ	0-310-20683-9
Community: Building Relationships Within God's Family	0-310-20677-4
Evangelism: Becoming Stronger Salt and Brighter Light	0-310-20678-2
Lessons on Love: Following Christ's Example	0-310-20680-4
Marriage: Building Real Intimacy	0-310-20675-8.
Parenthood: Rising to the Challenge of a Lifetime	0-310-20676-6
The Real You: Discovering Your Identity in Christ	0-310-20682-0
Character: Reclaiming Six Endangered Qualities	0-310-21716-4
Freedom: Breaking the Chains that Bind You	0-310-21717-2
Fruit of the Spirit: Living the Supernatural Life	0-310-21315-0
Jesus: Seeing Him More Clearly	0-310-21316-9
Prayer: Opening Your Heart to God	0-310-21714-8
Psalms: Deepening Your Relationship with God	0-310-21318-5
Transformation: Letting God Change You from the Inside Out	0-310-21317-7
Transparency: Discovering the Rewards of Truth-Telling	0-310-21715-6

*Look for Interactions at
your local Christian bookstore.*

WILLOW
Willow Creek Resources

www.willowcreek.com

ZONDERVAN™

GRAND RAPIDS, MICHIGAN 49530 USA

WWW.ZONDERVAN.COM

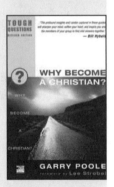

We want to hear from you. Please send your comments about this book to us in care of zreview@zondervan.com. Thank you.

GRAND RAPIDS, MICHIGAN 49530 USA

W W W . Z O N D E R V A N . C O M